D1450093

ARTISTS IN SPITE OF ART

ARTISTS IN SPITE OF ART

Ronald G. Carraher

VNR VAN NOSTRAND REINHOLD COMPANY
New York Cincinnati Toronto London Melbourne

Van Nostrand Reinhold Company Regional Offices:
New York Cincinnati Chicago Millbrae Dallas

Van Nostrand Reinhold Company International Offices:
London Toronto Melbourne

Designed by Ronald G. Carraher
Printed by Eastern Lithographing Corp.
Bound by Haddon Bindery, Inc.

Published by Van Nostrand Reinhold Company
450 West 33rd Street, New York, N.Y. 10001

Published simultaneously in Canada by
Van Nostrand Reinhold Company Ltd.

16 15 14 13 12 11 10 9 8 7 6 5 4 3 2 1

CREDITS

Every effort was made to obtain permission from the
artists whose works are reproduced; however, since most
naive art remains cloaked in anonymity, it was impossible
to properly credit all of the artists represented in this
collection. In the final section, however, I have been able
to credit several individual artists who are known for
having created many works over a period of time.

The captions serve only to identify the works, listing title
(by this author) and location and date when documenta-
tion photograph was made.

Photographs by the following photographers appear on
the pages indicated: Ralph Lapham, 14; Will Tebbs, 35;
Ed Kohnstamm, 85 (left); Donald Kottmann, 99, 100, 101,
102, 104, 105, 107; Nick Pavloff, 110.

Grave marker, Ronald, Washington, 1970

ACKNOWLEDGMENTS

In preparing this book I have been fortunate to have received the generous cooperation of many individuals who permitted me to photograph works of art which they owned or which they had created. A number of persons have directly or indirectly provided ideas and information that greatly enriched the concept of this collection.

Greg N. Blasdel wrote an excellent article entitled "The Grass-Roots Artist" for *Art in America,* documenting a number of important artists.

Willis Nelson, Ken Brandon, Donald Kottmann, J. Gary Brown, Thomas Elsner, and Sam Smidt were particularly helpful in sharing their views on this subject.

In gathering the material for this book I also had the inestimable advantage of suggestions and encouragement of my patient wife.

Ronald G. Carraher
Seattle, Washington

Chiropractor's office, San Francisco, California, 1967

INTRODUCTION

This book grew from the observation that a great many people without formal training in the arts produce vital and imaginative visual works. It is not essential that these efforts be considered art, although it is quite possible that the individuals who created the works are artists.

It would be convenient if the term "folk art" provided an adequate mental picture of these artists' statements. Terms such as "naive" and "primitive" are often used to describe a range of art from children's drawings to works having a special tribal origin; however, the examples presented in this collection are on the arcane periphery of traditional folk art. Lacking a precise historical definition, these pieces have been of little interest to museums or collectors. There are at present few publications devoted to them. Although any single classification for these works is inadequate, the term "naive" may be used to communicate some sense of the attitude of the artist.

Naive art is the record of an uncomplicated response. It cannot be learned, but it can be understood. The naive artist uses an unconscious and intuitive approach to the problem of communication. He does not disguise his techniques. He shares everything from the beginning. He works without concern for alternatives, and he has no fear of doing things poorly. He does not have to practice to improve. He willingly uses whatever materials are at hand to give form to his ideas. He is often more interested in his own creative process than in the finished product. His vernacular expression does not go through styles or fashion cycles since it is nearly immutable. His role as an artist may begin and end within the process of painting a single sign, or it may involve a lifelong dedication to a creative vision.

Since naive art is a rich source of conceptual ideas and unexpected visual forms, it is a valuable and inspirational resource for the practicing designer or artist. Pablo Picasso, Jean Dubuffet, Alexander Calder, and the late Ben Shahn are among the many contemporary artists whose painting and sculpture reflect a sensitivity to the attitudes and motifs of the untrained artist.

The following photographs and illustrations document some of the ways people have satisfied their need for creative self-expression. The images of this book are intended to introduce nonartists to themselves and encourage them to share with us their visual thoughts and fantasies.

An individual who would never claim any artistic aptitude will unhesitatingly undertake an elaborate sign-lettering project. The finished hand-painted sign, a manifestation of the American do-it-yourself tradition, composes an important category of naive art.

The homemade sign is an expected part of both urban and rural environments, and an afternoon drive in any direction will lead to an encounter with some form of folk graphics. Beyond the mundane literal information, "HOUSE FOR RENT," "WORMS," or "FREE PUPPIES," is a message of natural graphic wisdom and a unique expression of a love of letters. It becomes clear why the Greeks used the same word to describe both writing and drawing.

A careful study of the visual forms of naive signs reveals information about the process of creative invention as well as the personal values of the untrained artist. Alphabet letters derive from a formal tradition, and we generally experience them in the refined and structured context of the printed page. Creating a sign involves recalling this precise prototype and mustering sufficient dexterity to handle brush and paint. The results are as intimate and revealing as handwriting.

Changes in size and placement of letters may alter the expected meaning. A freedom from convention may lead to attempts to create a more decorative or ornamental letter-form. There is only a casual interest in the problem of consistency. An afterthought may add an element of surprise to an otherwise ordinary line of words. Individual letters are sometimes drawn with a halting, tactile kind of line that keeps perfect pace with the artist's vague recollection of the classical form.

Alphabet by old-age pensioner, Seattle, Washington, 1964

Alphabet by old-age pensioner (detail), Seattle, Washington, 1964

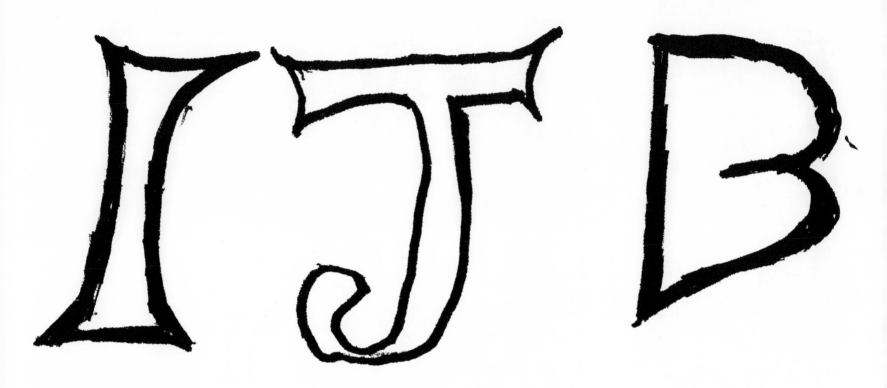

Alphabet by old-age pensioner (detail), Seattle, Washington, 1964

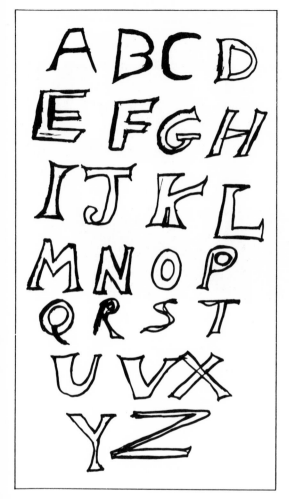

ABCD
EFGH
IJKL
MNOP
QRST
UVWX
YZ

Alphabet by old-age pensioner, Seattle, Washington, 1964

Times Roman Typeface

Fortunately, the alphabet can survive severe distortions and still maintain its graphic identity. The high energy level and inventive letter designs more than compensate for the obvious legibility problems. A naive sign at its best is a testimony to the artist's unshakable trust in the power of words.

A direct comparison with a formal typeface reveals the remarkable inventiveness of a naive alphabet. Each letter is individually shaped within a loose concern for overall style. The characters are at once forceful and vague.

Barber Shop, Seattle, Washington, 1966

Skating, Seattle, Washington, 1970

FideLity Printing

Fidelity Printing, California, 1966

Assorted mailboxes, northwestern United States, 1967

Uncle Sam mailbox, Washington, 1969

Painting the family name on the ungainly shape of a rural mailbox has generated a do-it-yourself tradition around the simple process of visual identification. When a number of mailboxes are compared, it is apparent that the hand-painted lettering invariably reveals individuality as well as a memorable word-image. The task poses a problem that cannot be avoided — it must be solved.

Fruit, Yakima, Washington, 1965

The fruitstand sign-maker is faced with the problem of creating a large number of ephemeral signs which must be continually changed to indicate new prices and seasonal produce. Although such signs may seem alike superficially, study and comparison reveal that many are graphically unique.

Strawberry Center, Gilroy, California, 1967

Ice Cold Watermelon, San Jose, California, 1968

We Quit, San Jose, California, 1958

17

Shoes, shirts, and toys, Seattle, Washington, 1969

Corsages, San Jose, California, 1967

Used rear ends, Spanaway, Washington, 1969

For Rent, San Jose, California, 1966

Shoetician, Washington, 1969

Golden Rule Food Company, Washington, 1970

Roadside zoos have almost been annihilated by limited-access freeways, but a few still survive in the Midwest. Their advertising is a vigorous combination of verbal and visual elements related to both the billboard tradition and carnival and sideshow graphics. Sometimes a score of such signs stretch across hundreds of miles in a sequence of related previews of the final attraction.

The owner of this Iowa reptile ranch has painted a classical "dangerous snake" as his tourist lure. The unpredictable curves of the snake are in total tension with the letters of the word "animal." The composition begins and ends with the tail, which doubles as a most effective pointing device.

Reptile Ranch, Clinton, Iowa, 1965

Photo Studio, Seattle, Washington, 1968

Ice, Rosalyn, Washington, 1970

Gas prices, Oak Harbor, Washington, 1969

Five Cents, Providence, Rhode Island, 1965

The naive sign painter shapes numbers with the same energy and love of form that characterize his designs for verbal messages.

Directives, warnings, and territorial markings often provoke a special interest in sign-making (opposite). The information of the sign is presented as a kind of barrier or protective device. To trespass these steps requires sitting on the sign.

Stay, Out, Seattle, Washington, 1970

No Sitting on These Steps, Seattle, Washington, 1968

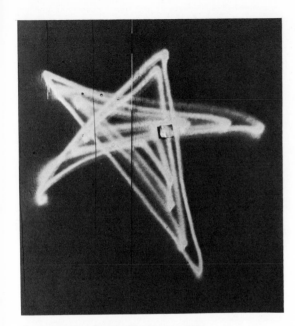

Spray-can star, Seattle, Washington, 1970

Protests of all kinds have given rise to a naive art of special emotional intensity. Placards and signs have become an expected part of the communication at such events. Protest graphics are often created on the spot with materials at hand, but their visual expression of deeply felt beliefs and concerns provides a memorable form of naive art.

Peace march sign, California, 1967

Protest car, San Francisco, California, 1967

Front porch protest, Seattle, Washington, 1970

27

True Love, San Jose, California, 1967

I Love . . .?, Seattle, Washington, 1969

Railroad underpass graffiti, Tacoma, Washington, 1968

This railroad overpass — decorated with what might be called group graffiti — is located near a large suburban high school. The nicknames and initials have been painted on the viaduct as part of what is seemingly a school tradition: adding your initials to the wall becomes a way of visually insuring that you are part of the group. Individuality of expression is less important than merely making a record of your participation.

Railroad underpass graffiti (detail), Tacoma, Washington, 1968

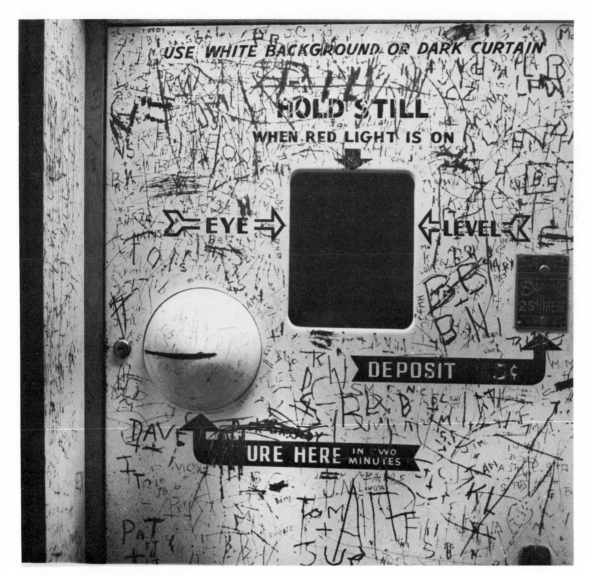

Photo booth interior, Seattle, Washington, 1953

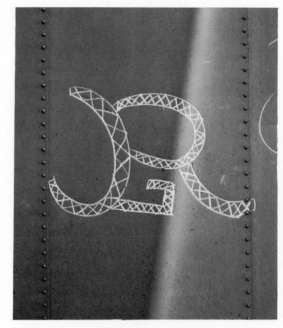

Monogram, Seattle, Washington, 1969

The "Kilroy was here" impulse motivates a kind of monogram graffiti (left) which may evolve into an elaborate letter-form design. The designer gives little thought to permanence, since the act of leaving a mark is the essential thing. This particular monogram (above) is chalked on the side of a railroad boxcar.

Since legibility is not often a primary concern of the naive sign painter, lettering (opposite) is frequently painted on surfaces that create a barely ordered chaos for the eye.

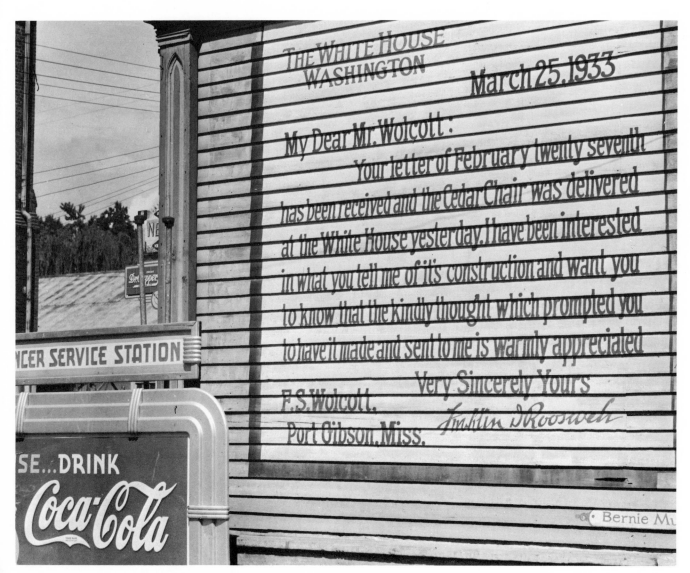

Facsimile of letter written by President Roosevelt to resident — painted on side of building. 1940. Photo: Marion Post Walcott for FSA. Courtesy Library of Congress.

Religious plaque, Monroe, Washington, 1969

Grassroots churches and other organizations
frequently rely upon the talents of member
volunteers for identifying signs. The graphic
results are sometimes a record of fervent feel-
ing, in this case religious. The amount of verbal
information does not dilute the impact of the
final presentation. The letters and words provide a focus for the faith that is needed to
transform a vacant storefront into a place of
worship.

Church of God, Washington, 1970

Church front, California, 1968

Now Open, Seattle, Washington, 1967

The problem of directing the movement or attention of others motivates a wide variety of graphic images utilized by the naive designer. Pointing hands, arrows, and gesturing figures are the graphic ingredients of this tradition of pointing devices. In spite of problems of proportion, redundancy, spacing, and rendering, these simple pointing devices seldom fail to function.

Although hands are difficult to draw, they are a popular subject for pointing the way. They offer a personalized visual imperative.

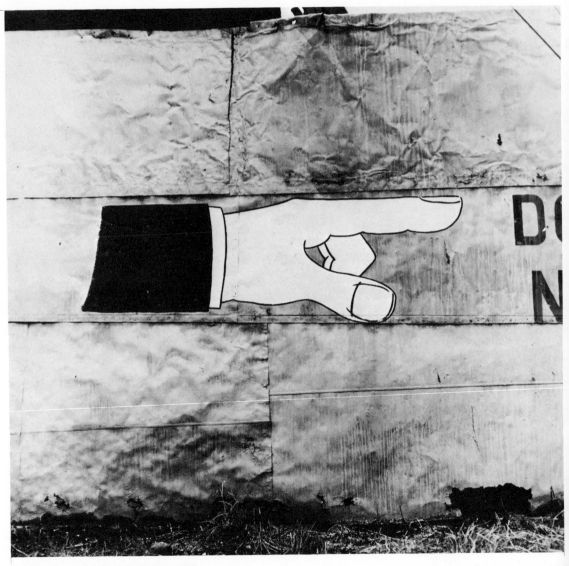

Pointing finger, Seattle, Washington, 1966

34

Rush, Omak, Washington, 1935

Entrance, Seattle, Washington, 1970

Please, Port Angeles, Washington, 1969

Man pointing, Freedom, California, 1967

Pay, Seattle, Washington, 1970

Service Center, Seattle, Washington, 1970

The arrow has a universal usefulness in directing attention and traffic. The form of the arrow survives unending manipulation at the hands of the naive sign-maker. Drawing an arrow that will direct people around a corner (opposite) is a challenge even for the professional designer. The problem never fails to call forth an inventive solution.

The roadside fireworks stand is a uniquely American structure. Often it is decorated with a spirit that exceeds the requirements of simple sign-making. The burning rocket on this stand (right) also functions as an effective pointing device.

Fireworks stand, Coyote, California, 1967

Around the Corner, Seattle, Washington, 1969

Spray-can arrow, Seattle, Washington, 1970

Green Thumb, Stevens Pass, Washington, 1970

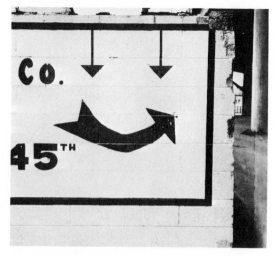

Down and around arrows, Seattle, Washington, 1969

Easy Shoppe, Washington, 1970

Tattoo shop window sign, Seattle, Washington, 1958

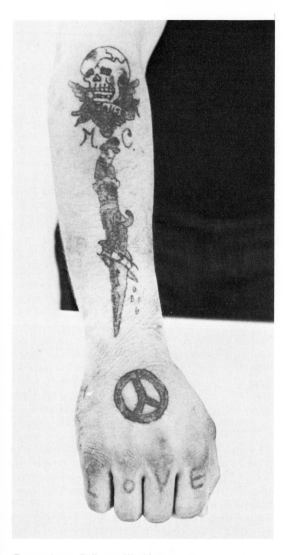

Tattoos appear in some form in nearly every culture and have highly developed historical precedents in countries such as Japan and New Zealand. In America, tattooing retains a certain folk-art or popular-art character. Its images are a curious blend of the Sunday comics, the Orient, and black magic. However primitive the concept may seem, tattooing is still practiced in nearly every major city. Patrons desiring a tattoo make their selection from one of dozens of style sheets that illustrate the repertoire of the shop owner. The tattooist outlines the design on the skin, inks it in, and completes his work with additional colors and shading.

Winged skull tattoo, San Jose, California, 1967

Tattooed arm, Bellevue, Washington, 1970

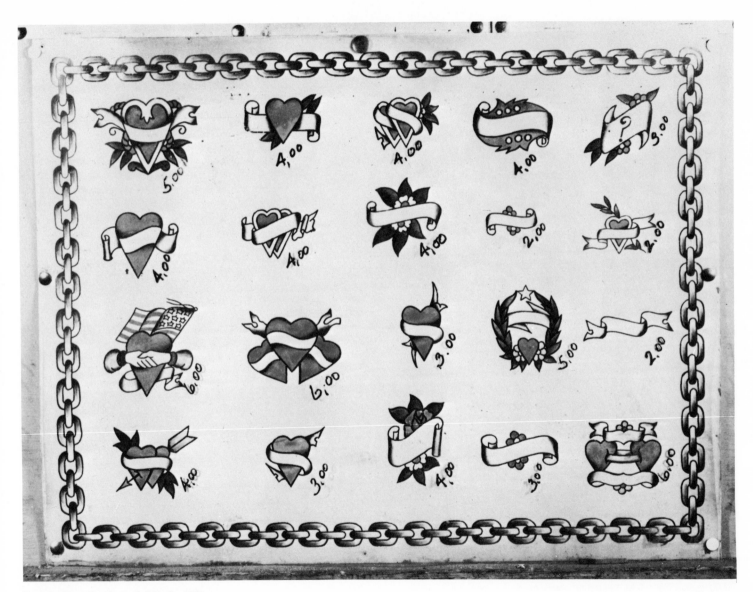

Heart tattoos, San Jose, California, 1967

Animal head tattoo, San Jose, California, 1967

Mother tattoo, San Jose, California, 1967

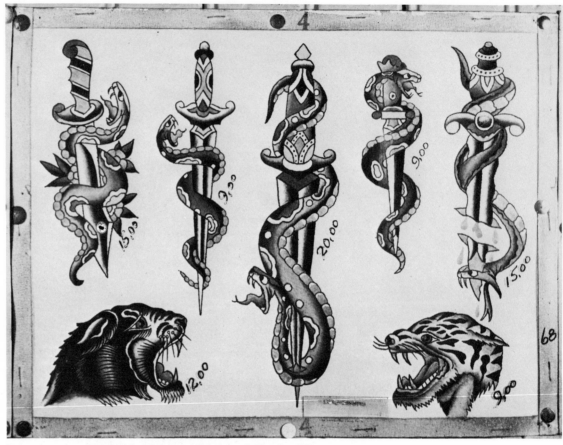

Daggers, snakes, and cats' heads tattoos, San Jose, California, 1967

Eagle tattoo, San Jose, California, 1967

Butterfly tattoo, San Jose, California 1967

Shark-girl tattoo, San Jose, California, 1967

Dragon tattoo, San Jose, California, 1967

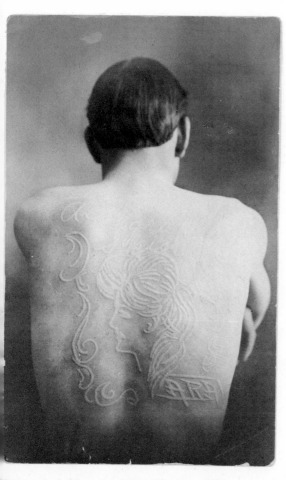

Autographed skin postcard, Iowa City, Iowa, 1891

A sharp stick was used to draw directly on the skin of this man's back, raising a red welt or temporary skin drawing. The use of unconventional materials in the "autographed skin" may be seen as an instance of the naive artist's willingness to work with even minimal resources.

Emblems or badges are, in a sense, cloth tattoos. Like tattoos, their design is stylized; they are characterized by heavy outlines and separated colors. They are sometimes worked out in sketch form by a member of an organization in search of a visual identification. The rough sketch is submitted to an emblem manufacturer, which leads to further alterations of the original image.

Army unit emblem collection, San Leandro, California, 1967

Patriots' jacket, Bellevue, Washington, 1970

Sweater emblem collection, San Jose, California, 1968

Teamster's sign, Seattle, Washington, 1968

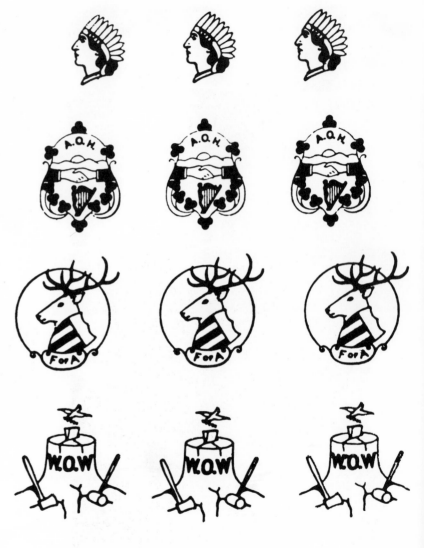

Fraternal emblems, Los Angeles, California, 1960

Hell's Rulers' jacket, Bellingham, Washington, 1970

Fraternal symbols, folk heraldics, and crests provide an outlet for the talents of the naive artist. The subject matter of such symbols is usually determined in part by some historical precedent and is then executed in accordance with real or supposed traditions by the designer. His attempt to make a painstakingly literal translation of the information may also include innovations and suggestions that come directly from members of the club.

Animals are popular subjects with obvious connections to the tradition of totems. A variety of subjects may be juxtaposed to emphasize symbolic meanings. Very often, scale relationships are freely altered to facilitate composing the elements.

After the basic design of the symbol or crest is determined, other members of the organization may decide to create their own interpretations for such specialized applications as an outdoor sign, place marking, or flag.

Skulls and crossbones, 1968

The skull-and-crossbones image is a highly specific visual message. Although everyone knows what its form is, naive attempts to draw it result in unique and individual interpretations. The essential form must survive the stylization, but the design cannot be merely copied. Interestingly, because the subject incorporates a *face* configuration, the final graphic form sometimes acquires a quality of self-portraiture.

Kindly Cooperate, Seattle, Washington, 1969

The custom-made rubber stamp often expresses a highly personal concept. Since professional artists are seldom involved in creating the design, the stamps may result in unexpected whimsy. Separated from their original functions, these stamps can be appreciated for their earnest visual form as well as their absurdity.

Rubber stamps are a favorite tool of the do-it-yourself artist. Anyone who has made a sign using a stamp-pad alphabet knows that the indelible redundant images encourage manipulation and graphic play.

Assorted rubber stamps, Seattle, Washington, 1969

Sore-feet display, San Jose, California, 1967

Some naive signs rely primarily on a graphic equivalent for an intended verbal meaning. The sign-maker may create a symbol that represents the service or goods of his business operation. These solutions have a sophisticated heritage in the wrought-iron sign-symbols of European shops and inns.

This model (above) made of carved plaster dramatizes a concern for sore feet. The message of this three-dimensional display requires no words.

Secondhand tires for sale, San Marcos, Texas, 1940. Photo: Russell Lee for FSA. Courtesy Library of Congress

Clenched fist, Seattle, Washington, 1969

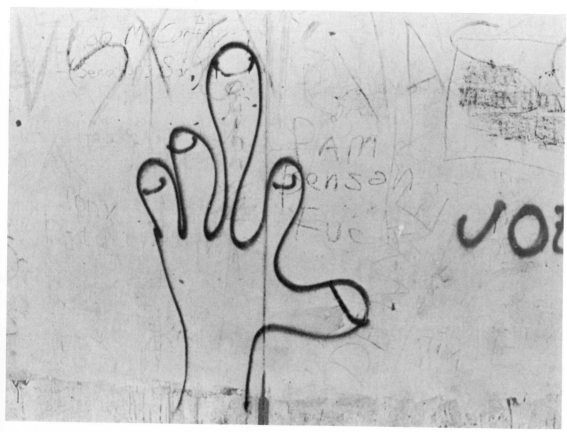

Hand, Santa Cruz, California, 1967

The can of spray paint has become another standard tool for the naive artist. It is ideal for instant lettering, providing a rapid flow of paint that has good coverage even on rough surfaces. The width of the spray requires a controlled and rhythmic movement of the arm for best results. As with many other projects, some pre-planning may be neded to maintain a coherent graphic form.

The clenched fist is drawn skillfully, with an economy of line that may be compared with some of today's most sophisticated corporate symbols.

There is an inherent play quality in naive art; thus, it is especially amusing when the art is applied to the business of play. Most of us have had some experience with amusement machines in a penny arcade. Although mass-produced commercial machines are replacing the traditional handcrafted amusement devices, many of the old prototypes are still in operation. The designer of these machines had not only to engineer the interior mechanical functions, but also had to create an exterior that would stimulate and intrigue potential customers. As a result, the tradition that developed was one of exaggerated style and visual hyperbole.

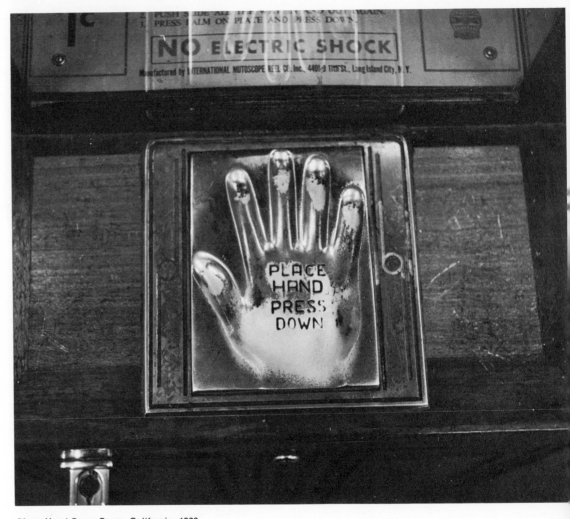

Place Hand Press Down, California, 1966

Wizard Fortune-Teller, California, 1965

Kiss-O-Meter, California, 1966

Within the larger tradition of amusement devices is the highly specialized concept of the shooting gallery. The format of the gallery presents an elegant distillation of function, fun, and the design process. The targets are realized in the familiar star and circle shapes and usually incorporate animal and human cutouts. In this example, the life-size figure of a man determines the entire composition of the gallery. All of the elements are cut from heavy sheet metal. After each week of firing-line activity, the gallery is completely repainted. Since the repainting process only casually repeats the previous week's patterns, the configuration of the colors is continually being redefined.

Shooting gallery, Rhode Island, 1965

Electric Energizer, California, 1964

Electric Energizer (detail), California, 1964

Fun house, Washington, 1968

Your Fortune by Cards, Rhode Island, 1964

Voo-Doo Child, California, 1968

Sideshow graphics are, in a way, a portable environment. They are an attempt to give visual form to the incredible. Information is deliberately manipulated to arouse the viewer's curiosity. The graphic style is never far from that of the circus poster.

Caged Gorilla, California, 1968

Thou Shalt Not Kill, Seattle, Washington, 1968

The process of personalizing a mass-produced object seems to hold a special fascination for naive artists, who frequently choose the automobile for embellishment. The resulting graphics are sometimes more than mere decoration: they may serve as a kind of public statement of the owner's beliefs and attitudes on social issues. The impulse may begin and end with a simple decal or bumper sticker — but for a more creative and determined individual the thought may resolve itself in a mural of images and words that cover the entire surface of the car.

The communication potential of such mobile graphics is best experienced in an environment of vehicles moving slowly through rush-hour traffic.

"Hep Cats" car, Louisville, Kentucky, 1940. Photo: Marion Post Walcott for FSA. Courtesy Library of Congress

Love car, North Bend, Washington, 1970

Love car (detail), North Bend, Washington, 1970

Psychedelic car, Seattle, Washington, 1962

MAKE LOVE NOT WAR

NNT 810

PEACE

Peace bus, San Francisco, California, 1967

Vegetable truck, San Jose, California, 1968

This communication potential is the basis for advertising on trucks. Although this kind of advertising usually is designed professionally, small companies often use their ingenuity to create advertising that can be very effective. Physical limitations seldom deter the naive artist. The difficulty of rendering this copy of a Rembrandt painting on a corrugated metal truck panel (right) was an accepted working condition for the sign painter. Copying the lettering from the cigar box is easily within the artist's range of skills; however, the faces and the figures are a more challenging problem.

This vintage truck (above) is still in daily use for door-to-door delivery of vegetables. The side panels are carefully painted with copies of popular nineteenth-century landscape paintings.

Cigar truck, Oakland, California, 1967

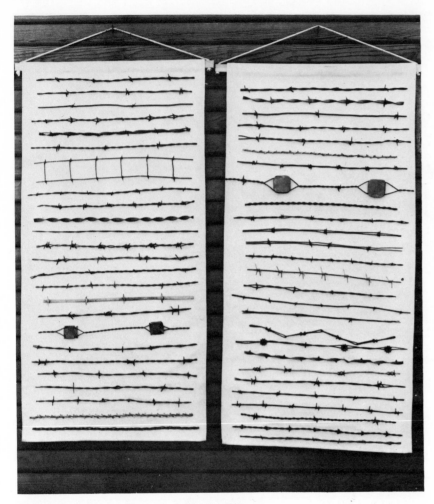

Barbed wire collection, Monterey, California, 1968

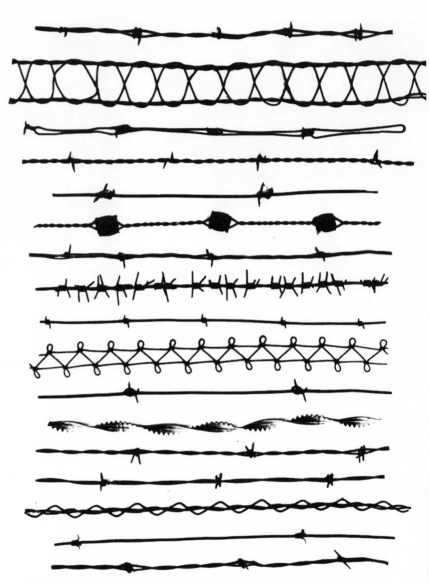

Barbed wire collection, Monterey, California, 1968

Collectors are a special group of naive artists. They devote a significant part of their lives to the process of gathering discarded objects and materials which they feel are beautiful, rare, or of special nostalgic value. When enough have been collected, they are sometimes assembled into a carefully planned formal presentation.

This collection of barbed wire (opposite) contains over five hundred different strands. The samples are cut in twelve-inch lengths and tied with nylon fish line on a series of canvas panels. The portable panels are transported to "meets" where other collectors gather to admire new finds and barter for extra samples.

These wire rug-beaters (right) were collected for their seemingly endless design variations. The linear elements are shaped in graceful patterns that obviously express more than mere functional requirements.

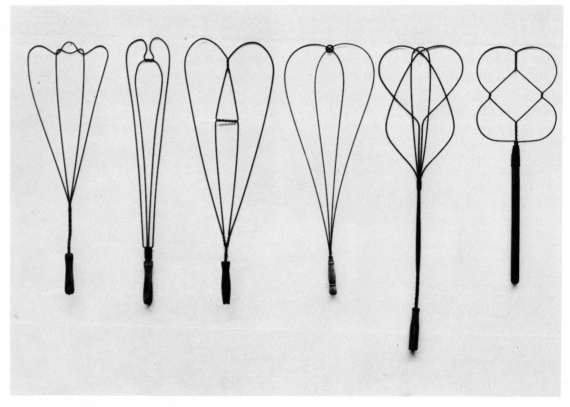

Rug beaters, Providence, Rhode Island, 1965

Occasionally, collected materials may inspire the collector to create some originals of his own design using the found objects in a new context. Discards are transformed into useful or decorative household accessories (right).

The mere availability of a raw material may provoke the naive artist to action. This picture frame (opposite) was assembled and carved from wood salvaged from cigar-box tops. The wooden lids were carefully stripped and notched before being laminated in a series of graduated layers.

Quilt made by Mrs. Bill Stagg, Pie Town, New Mexico, 1940. Photo: Russell Lee for FSA. Courtesy Library of Congress

Cigar-box picture frame, San Jose, California, 1967

Cigar-box picture frame, San Jose, California, 1967

Family-portrait coaster, Butte, Montana, 1965

Cigar-band bottle, San Jose, California, 1967

Family photographs are collected and treasured by almost everyone. Many people express their sentiment and nostalgia by making careful and considered presentations (left) of family album pictures, and this is yet another form of naive art. A naive artist does not hesitate to indulge emotions and feelings that others might judge trivial. His self-expression is open, personal, and without embarrassment. Weeks of work may be involved in creating a one-of-a-kind display such as these circular portrait coasters.

The desire to embellish and articulate the entire surface of an object is a universal impulse that has inspired some elegant tribal art. An object such as an ornately carved Polynesian canoe paddle is related at least in spirit to this naive presentative of a collection of cigar bands (left).

The bizarre ceramic ashtrays in this collection (opposite) are technically sophisticated, but their naive character endures. Circular openings in the figure are designed to accommodate matches and toothpicks. The walking legs are modestly wrapped in real ribbon.

This carved plaster shoe (opposite) is typical of the naive artist's fascination with visual contradictions. He often delights in designing objects with an unlikely form or function. The concern for details on the shoe far outweighs any interest in literal proportion or plausible scale.

Cigarette-girl dish, Newport, Rhode Island, 1964

Shoe ashtray, San Jose, California, 1965

Walking legs ashtray, Providence, Rhode Island, 1964

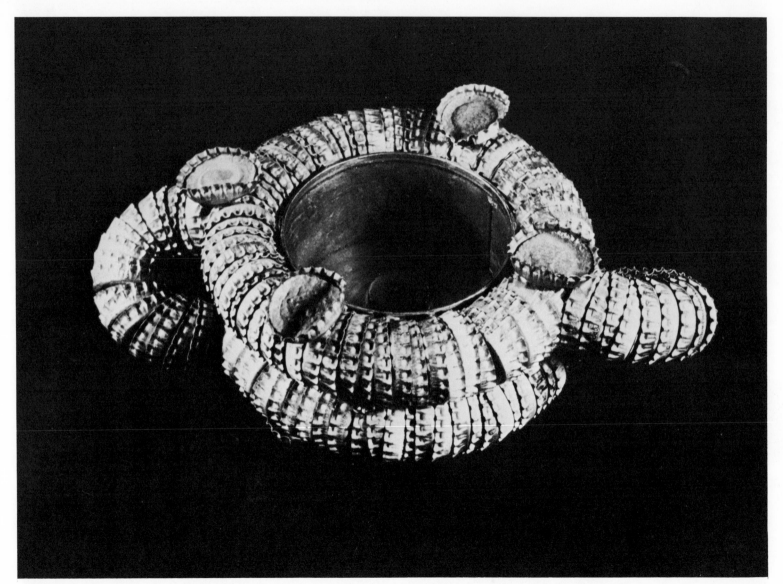

Bottle-cap ashtray, Redwood City, California, 1966

Trinkets in agricultural worker's automobile, Wilder, Idaho, 1941. Photo: Russell Lee for FSA. Courtesy Library of Congress

Weather vanes and wind mobiles, Seattle, Washington, 1970

Weather vane, Seattle, Washington, 1970

The naive artist often takes inspiration from unconventional found objects. These weather vanes were constructed from discarded refrigerator trays, muffin pans, and tin cans. The artist offered this comment: "I was mainly interested in making one that would spin without any special attention. Two of these have been going now for five years. Some of them aren't balanced that well."

Weather vane, Seattle, Washington, 1970

Flying duck, Seattle, Washington, 1970

79

Father and family, Oakland, California, 1968

These are two of the numerous constructions that appear and disappear along a tideland beach on San Francisco Bay. The driftwood is available in great quantity for any artist or group interested in building a temporary monument. From an adjacent freeway, thousands of passing spectators can observe the old structures being reassembled to create new sculpture.

The peace symbol is unique in that it was originally drawn by a professional designer; but it has since become a kind of international sign. It lends itself perfectly to translation and probably is reproduced more often than any symbol of the present day.

Peace symbol, Oakland, California, 1968

Cats' heads, Los Angeles, California, 1969

The urban environment supplies an assortment of ready-made formats. Once one artist makes the first discovery, his visual statement may trigger an endless dialogue of spontaneous variations.

This cat's head is one of many which appear and disappear on the metal flood-control gates in the canals around the Los Angeles area. The metal gate is only by chance shaped like a cat's head. During the dry season, when the gates are fully accessible, they are used for what could be considered a kind of completion painting project. Children and adults living nearby paint their interpretation of the basic theme within the metal outline. The drawings are visible for some distance, since the actual height of each head is over five feet. Commuters driving along the freeway can risk looking over, if they wish, to compare ten to twenty different versions in a sixty-mile-an-hour graphic exhibition.

Cats' heads, Los Angeles, California, 1969

Cat's head, Los Angeles, California, 1969

Palm tree mural, California, 1967

An outdoor wall mural can bring some cheer to a deteriorated environment. The dwelling on the back of this business building is enriched with a super-graphic treatment of palm trees, beaches, and ocean waves in full color.

Traditionally, the effigy is a crude image or figure representing someone or something that is the object of hatred or disgrace. It may also serve as a symbol for groups of people or institutions.

Hanging the coach in effigy (opposite) is almost as seasonal as the sport of football. The effigy is often the pet project of a group of disgruntled fans. The basic body is formed with stuffed clothing, with additional details added to the face and hands. The final figure is best understood in its role as a prop in a larger dialogue.

The scarecrow or harvest figure was originally erected to ward off predatory birds, but the decorative and ritual value of such figures has helped perpetuate the tradition (opposite).

Coach in effigy, Washington, 1968

Harvest figure, Half Moon Bay, California, 1967

Goodwill doll, Seattle, Washington, 1970

Girl , cocktail bar sign, California, 1967

Maria cocktail bar sign, California, 1967

Maria (detail) *cocktail bar sign,* California, 1967

The Christmas holidays encourage a nation-wide participation by naive artists as elaborate figures and intricate lighting displays appear on rooftops across the country. Each Christmas this display is prepared by a retired rancher. The figure of Santa Claus, balanced in the top of the tree, is holding a neatly wrapped gift. A variety of glass and plastic nonreturnable bottles is used to ornament the ends of the branches. The ladder is kept within easy reach for both the installation and removal of Santa.

Santa Claus tree, California, 1965

Barber shop window, Washington, 1967

This barber shop display is used as a traffic-stopper. The chair is about twice life-size; the barber is about three feet tall. The memorability of this still life depends in part on our universal fascination with all things miniature and gigantic.

Field figures, Santa Cruz, California, 1966

It is inevitable that some of the naive artist's activities defy explanation. These rows of figures might be scarecrows. They are located in a plowed field near a farm — but nothing is planted in the field. Each stake supports a burlap sack and a discarded hubcap. They are there because the artist wants them there.

Field figures (detail), Santa Cruz, California, 1966

Scarecrow, Duval, Washington, 1970

Indian with bow, Snoqualmie Pass, Washington, 1970

Indian with braids, Snoqualmie Pass, Washington, 1970

Indian with raised arm, Stevens Pass, Washington, 1970

The naive artist may be influenced in his work by some knowledge of certain art prototypes. These "cigar-store" Indians (opposite) were carved by a retired pensioner whose designs reveal a general familiarity with the historical style and pose of figures. The life-size carvings are detailed in bright enamel colors.

Most bakeries stock a wide selection of wedding cake figures. Subtle variations in the design and mood of these figures reveal them as an interesting indulgence of the naive artist. Their small scale and anonymous pose does not diminish their power as good-luck charms and symbols for the wedding ceremony. Although the figures are a commercial product, they are also a baker's work of art. Their outdated fashions and stoic expression make them a distant cousin of the cigar-store Indian.

Wedding cake figures, San Francisco, California, 1964

Pioneer figure, Eaglemount Rockeries, Port Townsend, Washington, 1970

These cowboy and Indian figures are part of a permanent roadside display. The bodies, composed of actual clothes and precast features, are assembled on a wire armature. Passing travelers are invited to stop and enjoy the figure groupings, which illustrate themes of brotherhood and early frontier life.

Indians, Eaglemount Rockeries, Port Townsend, Washington, 1970

Mt. Rushmore, Eaglemount Rockeries, Port Townsend, Washington, 1970

The faces on this artist's version of the Mt. Rushmore memorial were sculptured directly in a mound of cement. A natural rock provides a permanent pedestal.

Mt. Rushmore (detail), Eaglemount Rockeries, Port Townsend, Washington, 1970

Castle, Eaglemount Rockeries, Port Townsend, Washington, 1969

Yard sculpture often gets its start as a simple yard beautification project. Purely decorative fountains, walks, and arbors can evolve into elaborate outdoor displays. The satisfaction of creating a lilliputian rock castle may prove to be the beginning for an entire city in miniature.

A great many people make some gesture at personalizing their yards. It takes special courage, however, to use an entire outdoor area as a setting for a series of "wonders of the world revisited."

Sphinx, Eaglemount Rockeries, Port Townsend, Washington, 1969

Airplane, Thurwachter Ranch, Watsonville, California, 1968

Thurwachter Ranch, Watsonville, California, 1968

There are numerous examples of hedge sculpture, or topiary art, in the formal gardens of the world, but it is surprising to find these skillfully designed hedge trees in an agricultural setting near Watsonville, California. Their rounded forms loom up in startling contrast to the flat cultivated fields. Years of careful trimming were required to create the present sculptural reliefs. Although topiary art is most often associated with an impersonal and predictable decorative subject such as a swan or a geometric pattern, this artist has chosen to mold the hedge forms into more vernacular objects — patriotic stars, family names, and even a commemorative design of Lindbergh's airplane.

The naive artist often values his art as a means of making social contact with others. He doesn't hesitate to put his work on display, and his front yard is regularly used for this purpose. He is confident about the meaning of his art, and he is anxious to share it with the public.

Thurwachter Ranch, Watsonville, California, 1968

Thurwachter Ranch, Watsonville, California, 1968

Name plate, by Ed Root, Wilson, Kansas, 1968

Mosaic, by Ed Root, Wilson, Kansas, 1968

The work of most naive artists is by nature occasional. For some, a single hand-lettered sign may mark their only attempt at visual self-expression. For this reason most of the examples considered thus far have been both ephemeral and anonymous.

In addition to the "occasional" artists, however, there are a few individuals whose life-long involvement in the folk-art tradition deserves special attention. These naive "masters" are artists whose dedication and passion for self-expression have resulted in some remarkable creative achievements.

Ed Root of Wilson, Kansas, devoted nearly half of his ninety-two years to creating dozens of concrete yard sculptures, light fixtures, plaques, and planters. His cast-cement forms are richly surfaced with embedded bits of broken glass, tile, and found objects. Some of the larger forms are hollow and contain displays which can be viewed through small concealed openings.

Weather vane, by Ed Root, Wilson, Kansas, 1968

Dog and doghouse, by Ed Root, Wilson, Kansas, 1968

Yard sculpture, by Ed Root, Wilson, Kansas, 1968

Wind mobile, by Dave Woods, Humboldt, Kansas, 1968

Dave Woods lives near Humboldt, Kansas. In the 1950s he retired from a brick factory to use his time to create a personal visual environment. His art is created from neighbors' discards such as venetian blind slats, rubber tricycle tires, bedsprings, painted bottles, and broken lawn mowers. The objects are altered or joined to create environmental furniture, assemblages, wind machines, swings, and fences. Each new acquisition is given days of consideration and trial placements before being added to the existing works.

Lawn swing, by Dave Woods, Humboldt, Kansas, 1968

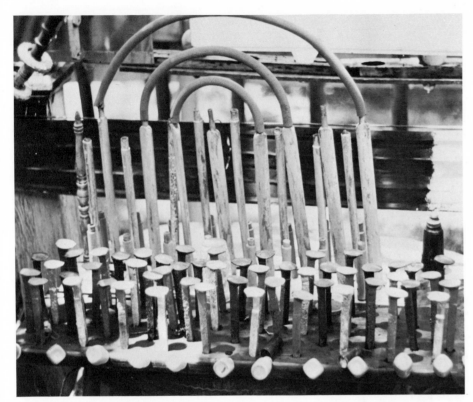

Railroad spikes, broom handles, and garden hose, by Dave Woods, Humboldt, Kansas, 1968

Car bumpers, by Dave Woods, Humboldt, Kansas, 1968

Devil, by S. P. Dinsmoor, Lucas, Kansas, 1969

Stone log cabin, by S. P. Dinsmoor, Lucas, Kansas, 1969

Not many artists — naive or professional — devote an entire lifetime to a single project. The "Garden of Eden" in Lucas, Kansas, is a monument to a rare kind of creative endurance. Although the project was never actually completed, S. P. Dinsmoor worked for over fifty years on an environmental sculpture that involved designing and constructing cement buildings, life-size trees and figures, a mauso-leum, and cement replicas of the American flag. The size and complexity of the Garden of Eden can only be compared to the more recent Watts Towers monument constructed by Simon Rodia in Los Angeles, California. In both the Watts Towers and the Garden of Eden, the artists chose to create their linear structures using reinforced cement. Maximum flexibility of design was possible with this inexpensive material that could be prepared as time and funds permitted.

Mr. Dinsmoor wrote a detailed account of his works in a booklet entitled *Pictorial History of the Cabin Home in the Garden of Eden.* The following selections from his writing reveal how he viewed his life style, the concept, and the finished work.

Flag, trees, and figures (detail), by S. P. Dinsmoor, Lucas, Kansas, 1969

This is the first flag ever made of concrete, I believe. It is 4x7 feet. It was made 15 years ago, placed on a cement tree above the trust. It has stood the test of storms for 15 years without falling or without a flaw. I thing it would be a great advantage to the government if they would put up cement flags, ball-bearing as this is, over lighthouses and other places where a permanent flag is wanted. It would stand out in plain view in all kinds of weather and could be seen where a cloth flag could not be seen.

From: *The Pictorial History of the Cabin Home in the Garden of Eden,* by S. P. Dinsmoor.

Flag, trees, and figures, by S. P. Dinsmoor, Lucas, Kansas, 1969

Mausoleum (detail), by S. P. Dinsmoor, Lucas, Kansas, 1969

Mausoleum, by S. P. Dinsmoor, Lucas, Kansas, 1969

Adam and Eve, by S. P. Dinsmoor, Lucas, Kansas, 1969

Cain and Wife, by S. P. Dinsmoor, Lucas, Kansas, 1969

Labor Crucified, by S. P. Dinsmoor, Lucas, Kansas, 1969

This is my coal house and ash pit, with Labor crucified above. I believe Labor has been crucified between a thousand grafters ever since Labor begun, but I could not put them all up, so I have put up the leaders—Lawyer, Doctor, Preacher and Banker. I do not say they are all grafters, but I do say they are the leaders of all who eat cake by the sweat of the other fellow's face. The Lawyer interprets the law. The Doctor has his knife and saw ready to carve up the bones. The Preacher is saying to this poor fellow crucified, "Never mind your suffering here on earth, my friend, never mind your suffering here, secure home in heaven for A-l-l E-t-e-r-n-i-t-y and you'll be all right." This is the stuff he is giving Labor for his cake. He knows nothing about Eternity and that he does know if he knows anything. What fools we be to sweat to give the other fellow cake. The Banker has the money, takes the interest and breaks up more people than any other class.

From: *The Pictorial History of the Cabin Home in the Garden of Eden,* by S. P. Dinsmoor.

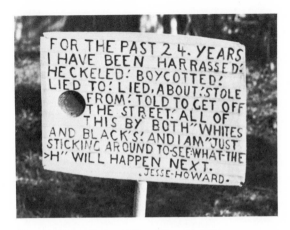

Signs, by Jesse Fuller, Fulton, Missouri, 1969

Personal philosophy and political beliefs often motivate the naive artist to use his art as a means of one-to-one communication. Jesse Fuller has surrounded his farm with signs that proclaim his views and concerns. The signs are occasionally stolen and they weather in time, but they are repainted and new thoughts are added, keeping the project alive. Individual words and ideas are emphasized by changes in size and through a personal kind of color coding.

Sign, by Jesse Fuller, Fulton, Missouri, 1969

Signs, by Jesse Fuller, Fulton, Missouri, 1969

Along one of San Francisco's crowded residential streets is this breathing space of brightly colored signs. It is a private garden full of painted sculpture and lively slogans proclaiming messages such as "Love thy neighbor" and "Wake up America." The project is the work of Peter M. Bond, a ninety-year-old philosopher and artist, who paints the signs in his basement studio. The garden is a visual presentation of a philosophic system about which he has written a book and numerous pamphlets.

Naive art can offer both the viewer and the artist an occasion for contemplation. We cannot predict when or where it will appear, but of one thing we can be certain: there undoubtedly will always be people who feel the need to make something original, and their work will always enliven and humanize the environment.

Pemabo Peace Garden, by Peter M. Bond, San Francisco, California, 1969

110

Pemabo Peace Garden, by Peter M. Bond, San Francisco, California, 1969

Pemabo peace garden, by Peter M. Bond, San Francisco, California, 1969

Donation container, Eaglemount Rockeries, Port Townsend, Washington, 1969